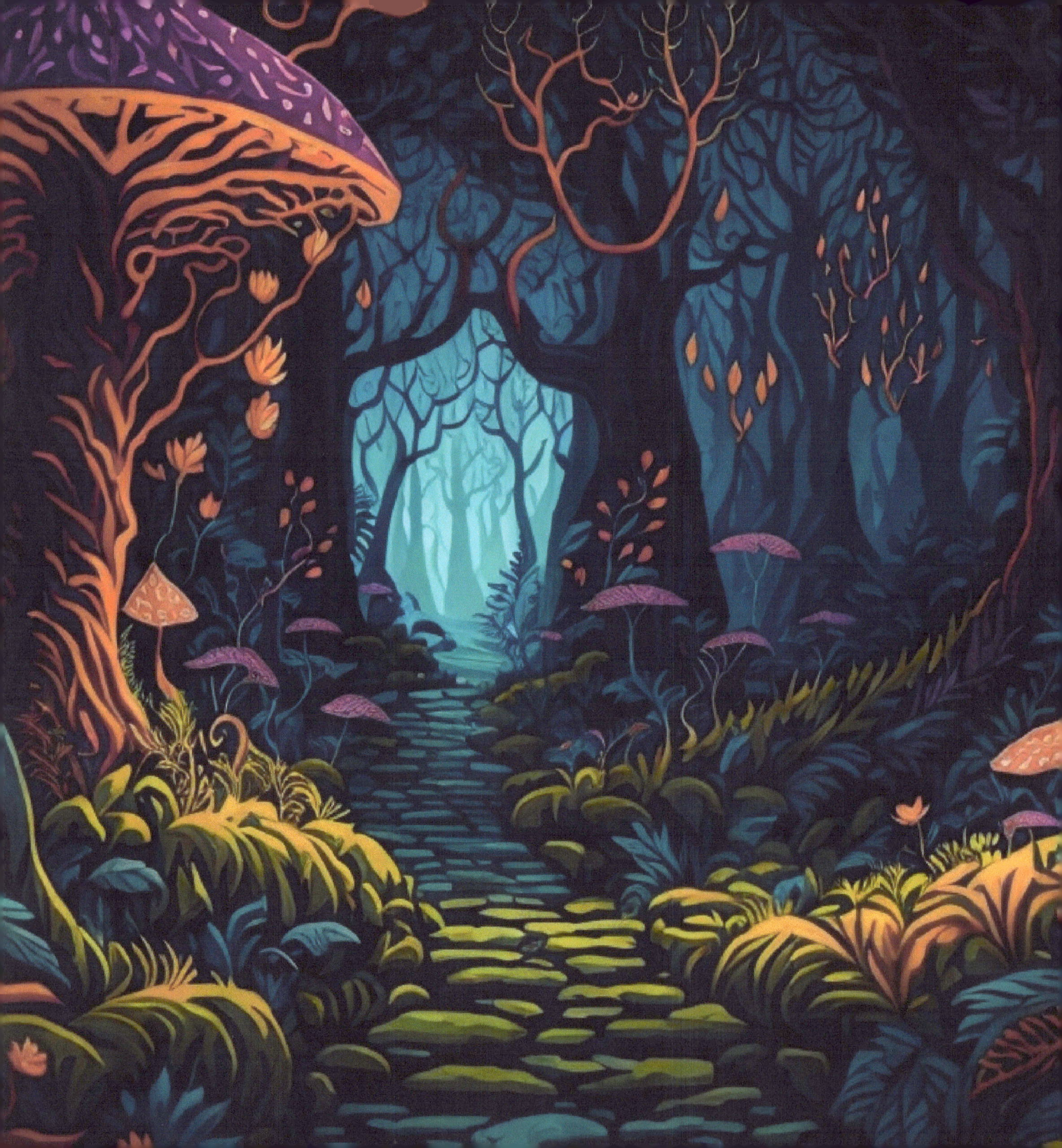

The Enchanted Forest

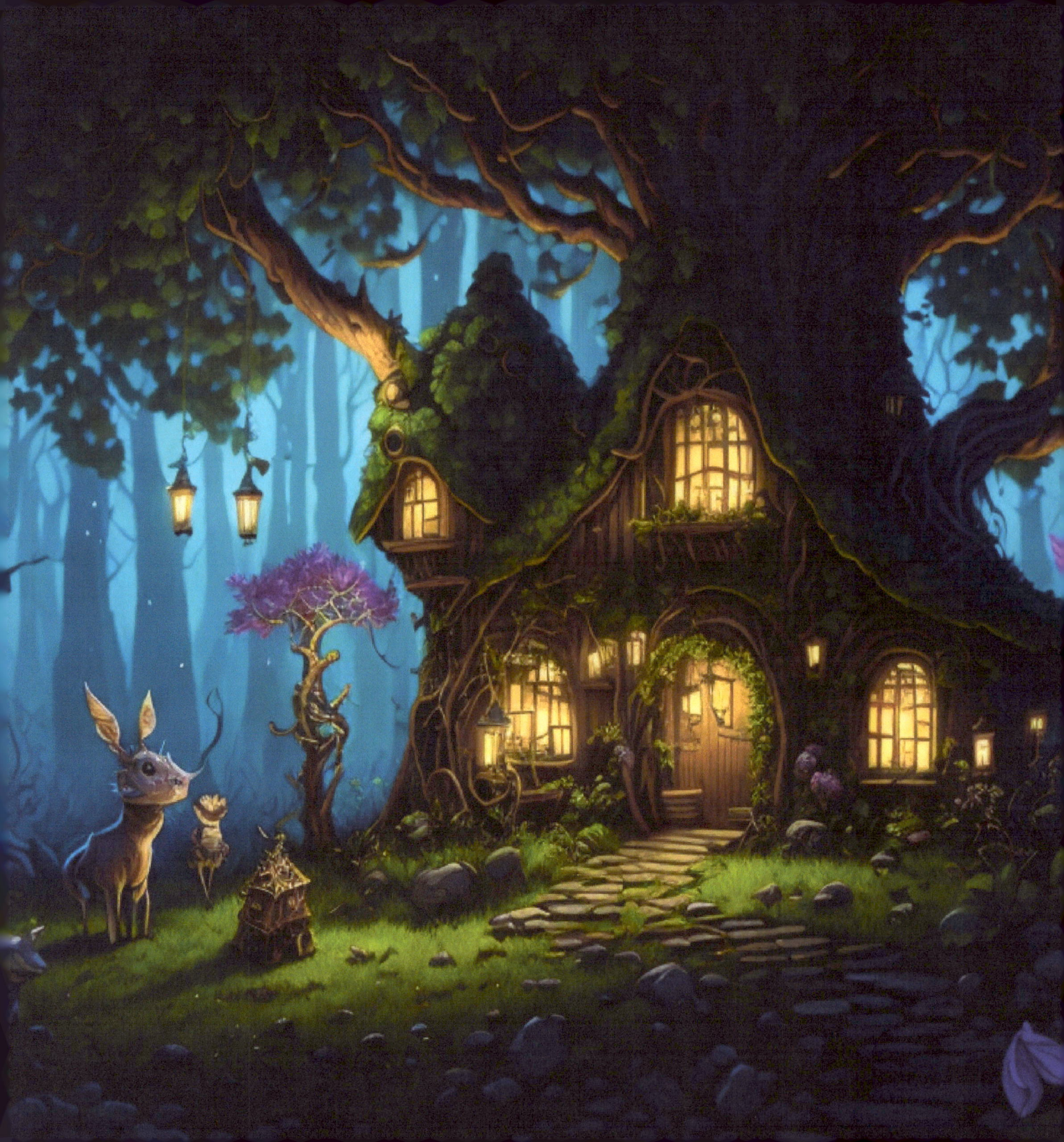

In the heart of an enchanted forest, Willow and Wanda, two young witches, live in a magical home. With whimsical surroundings and peculiar creatures, the forest sets the stage for their adventures. The mischievous duo explores the magical world, encountering talking trees and friendly pixies. As they navigate their enchanted home, readers are introduced to the rules and wonders of this mystical realm.

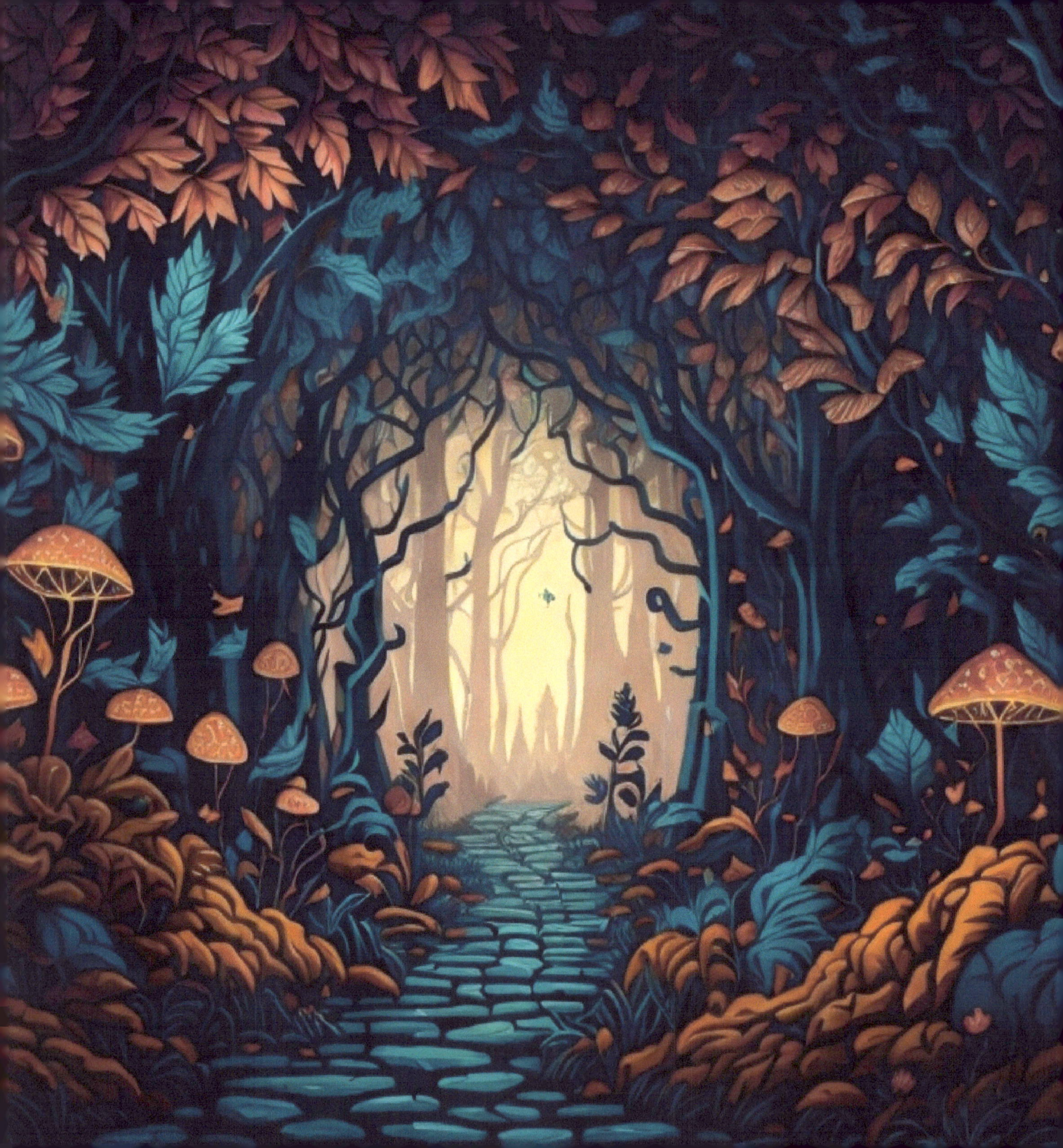

The Potion

Pranks

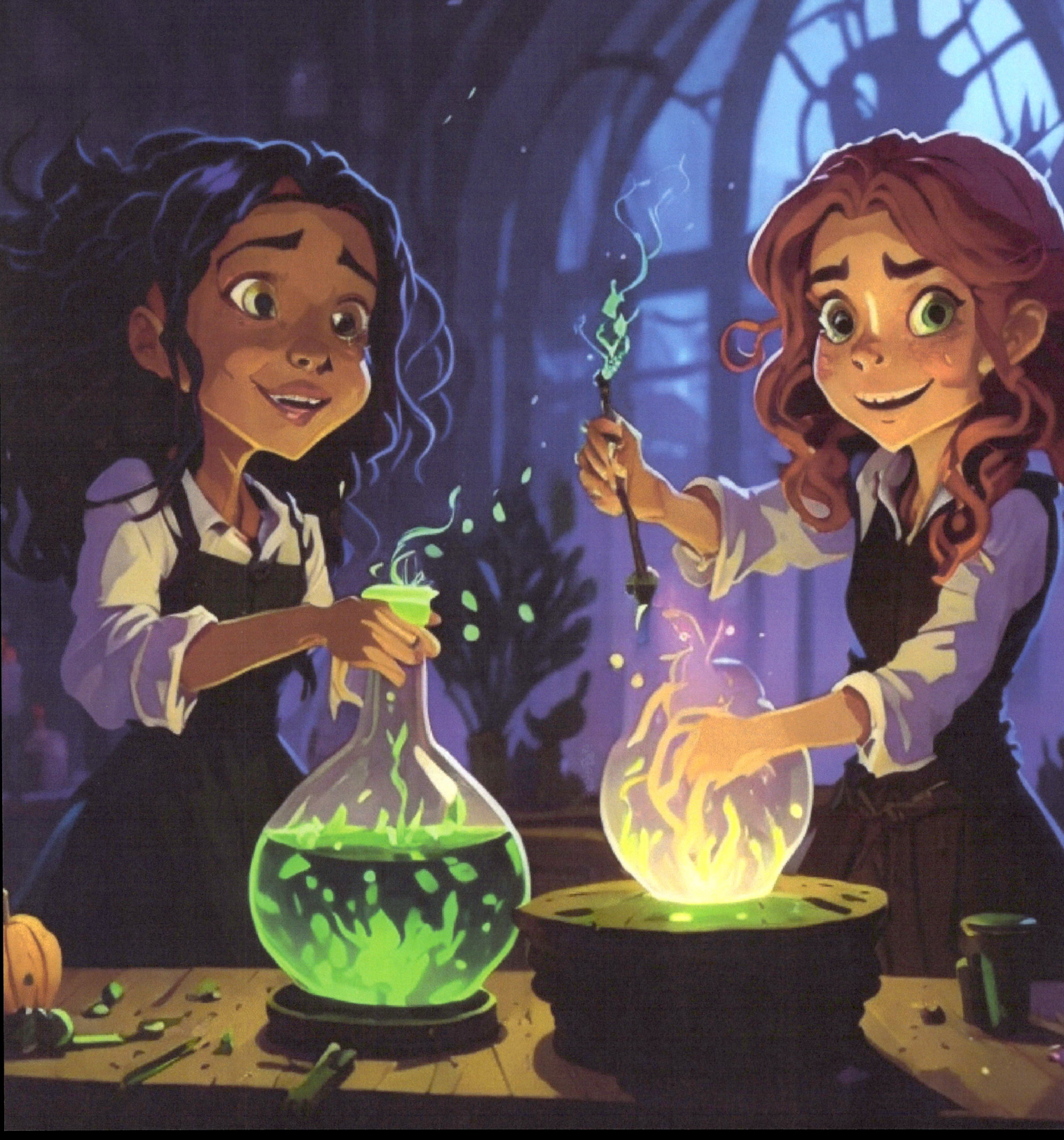

Attending a magical school, Willow and Wanda delve into the art of potion-making. Eager to showcase their skills, the witches decide to create a new potion, leading to unexpected and comical consequences. Bubbling cauldrons, magical mishaps, and laughter fill the potion-making class. The headmistress, a wise old witch, warns them about the importance of understanding magic fully. This chapter sets the stage for the mischievous nature of our magical protagonists.

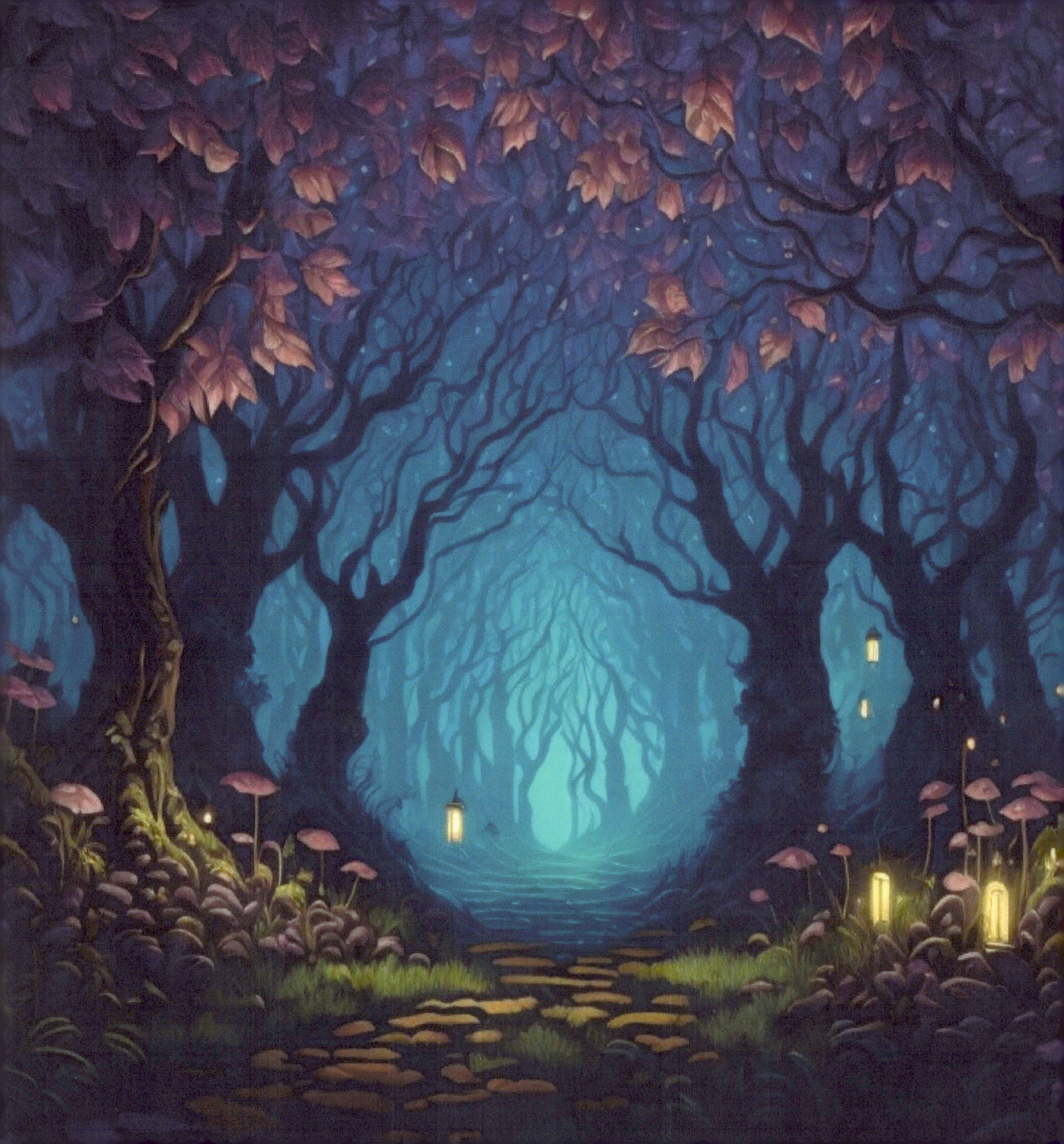

Broomstick

Ballet

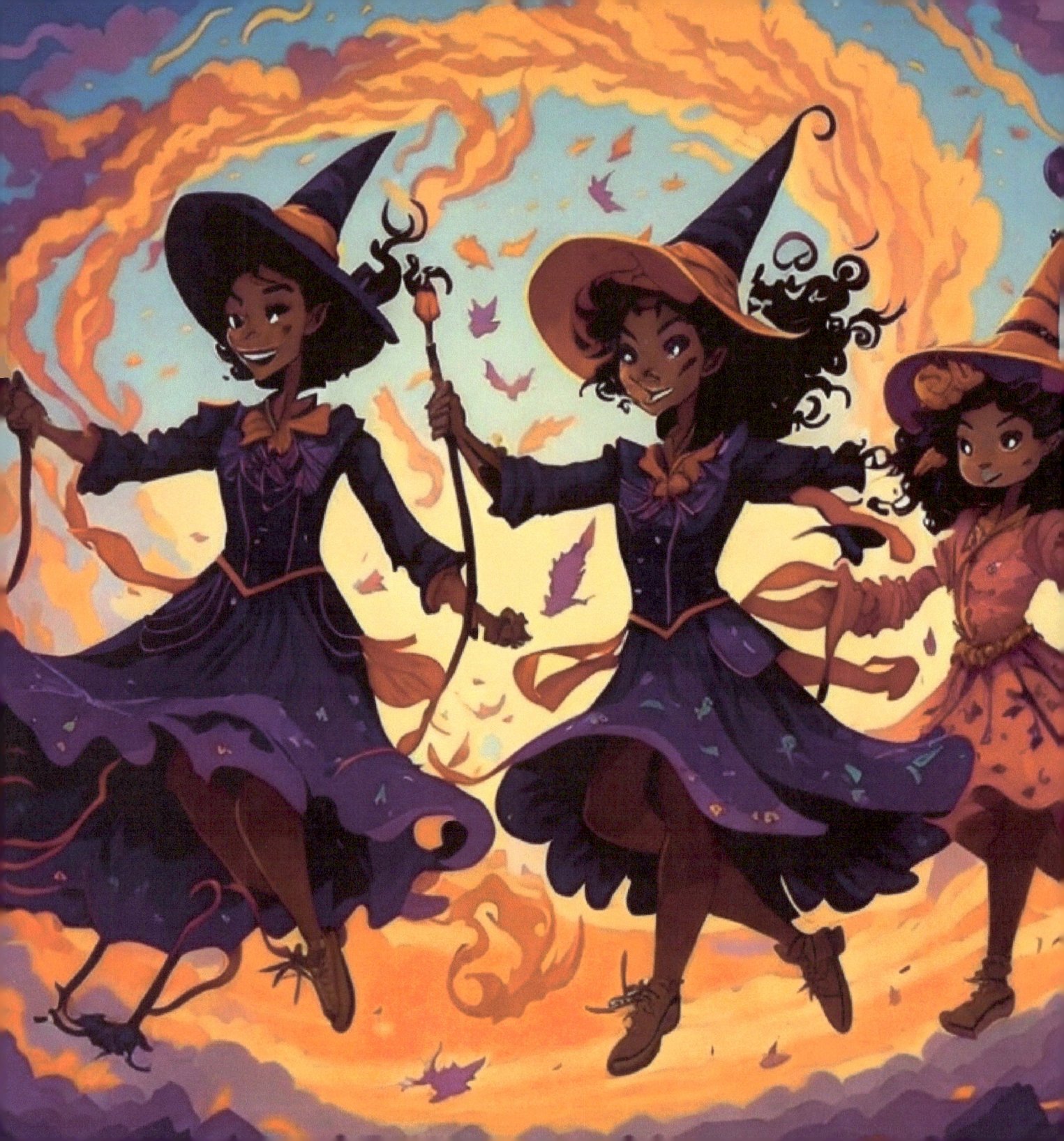

The annual Broomstick Ballet competition arrives, and Willow and Wanda are determined to participate. Their flying skills, though unconventional, provide entertainment as they twirl and twist through the sky. The chapter highlights the witches' playful nature and introduces other magical characters. Despite the chaos, the experience teaches them the value of teamwork, setting the tone for future adventures.

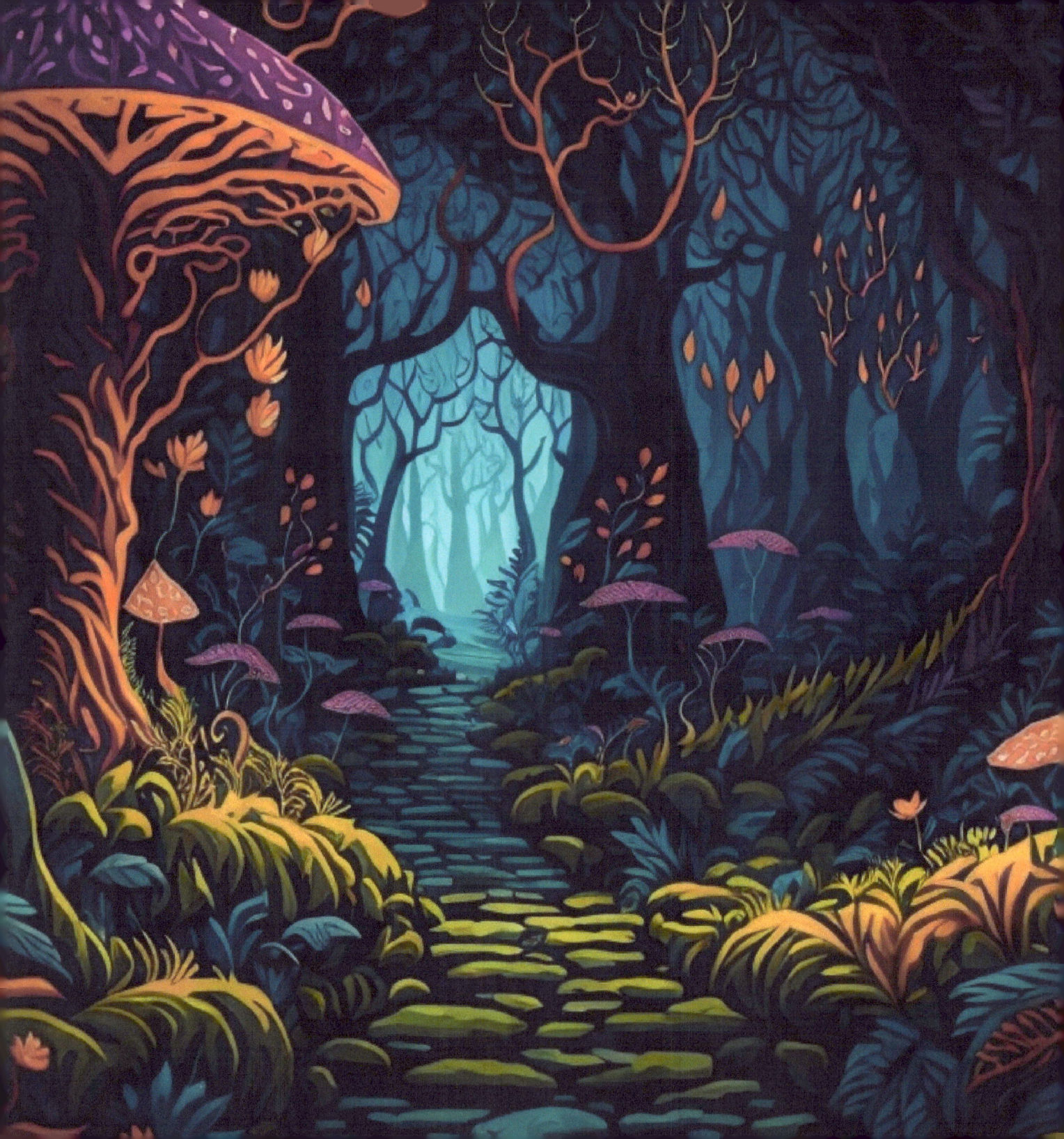

The Mysterious Spell Book

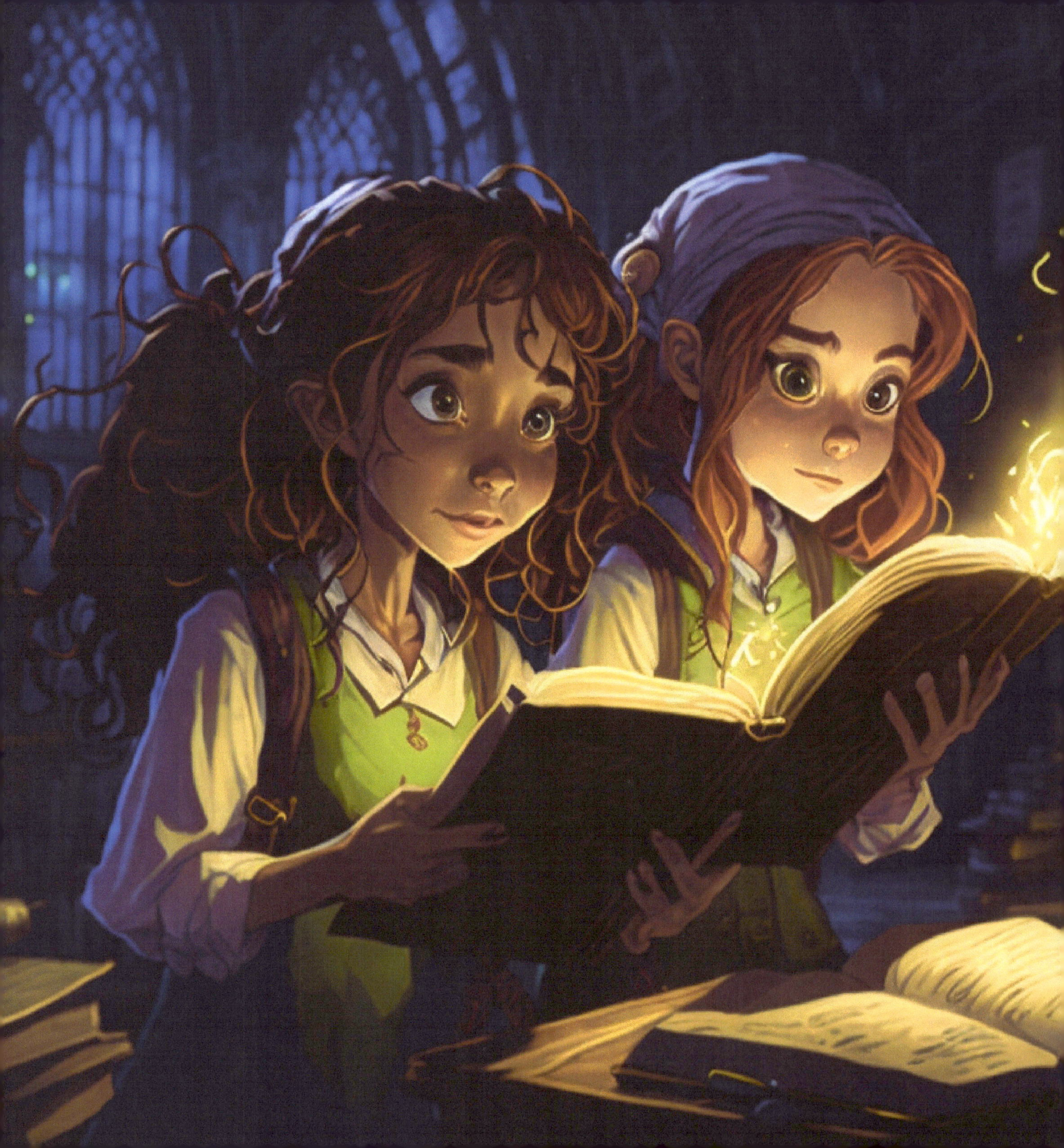

Curiosity gets the better of Willow and Wanda as they discover an ancient spell book in the restricted section of the school library. Tempted by the allure of powerful spells, they experiment without understanding the consequences. A mischievous magical creature is accidentally created, setting off a chain of events. The witches learn a valuable lesson about the responsibility that comes with wielding magical powers.

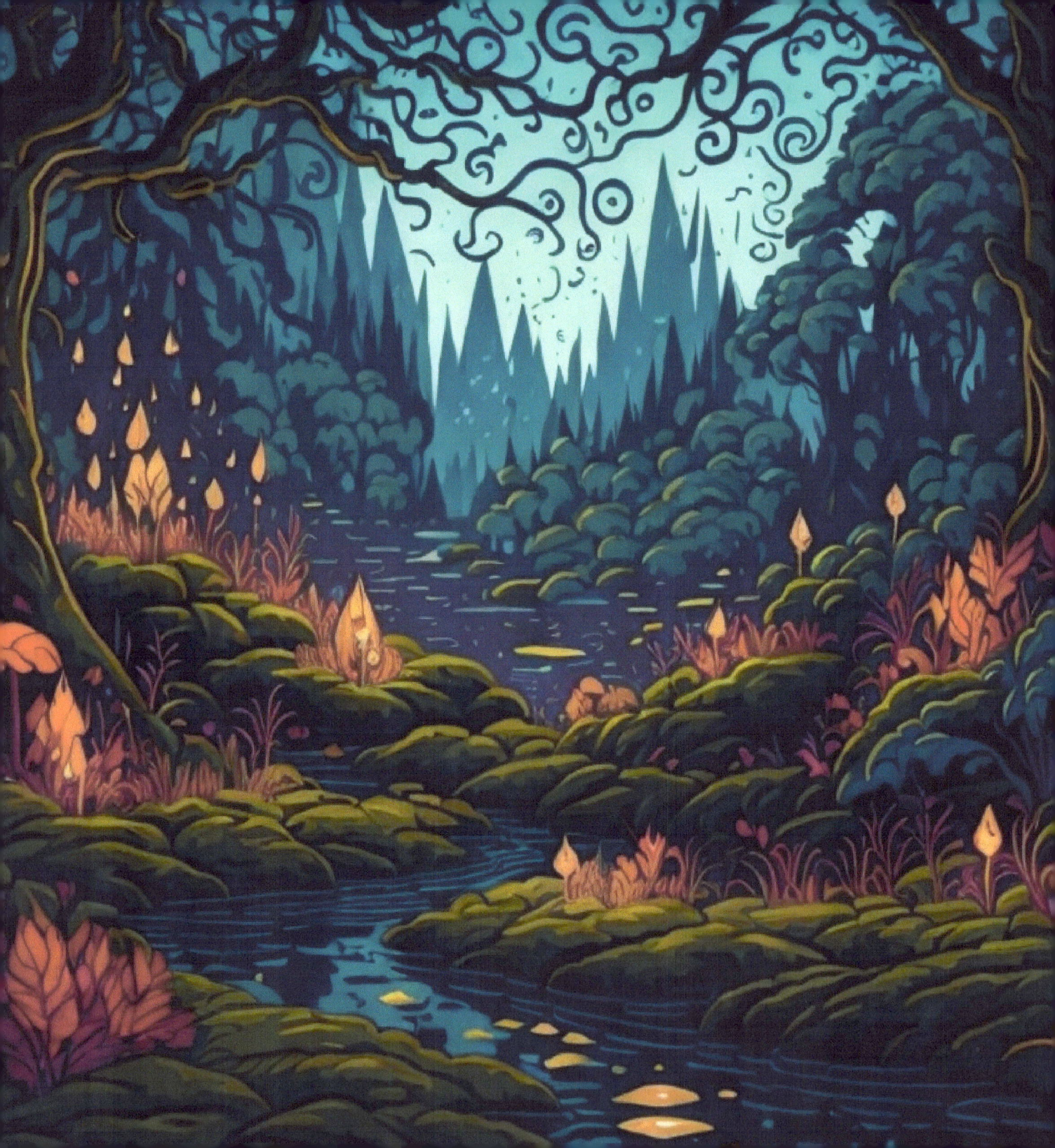

The Quest for a Solution

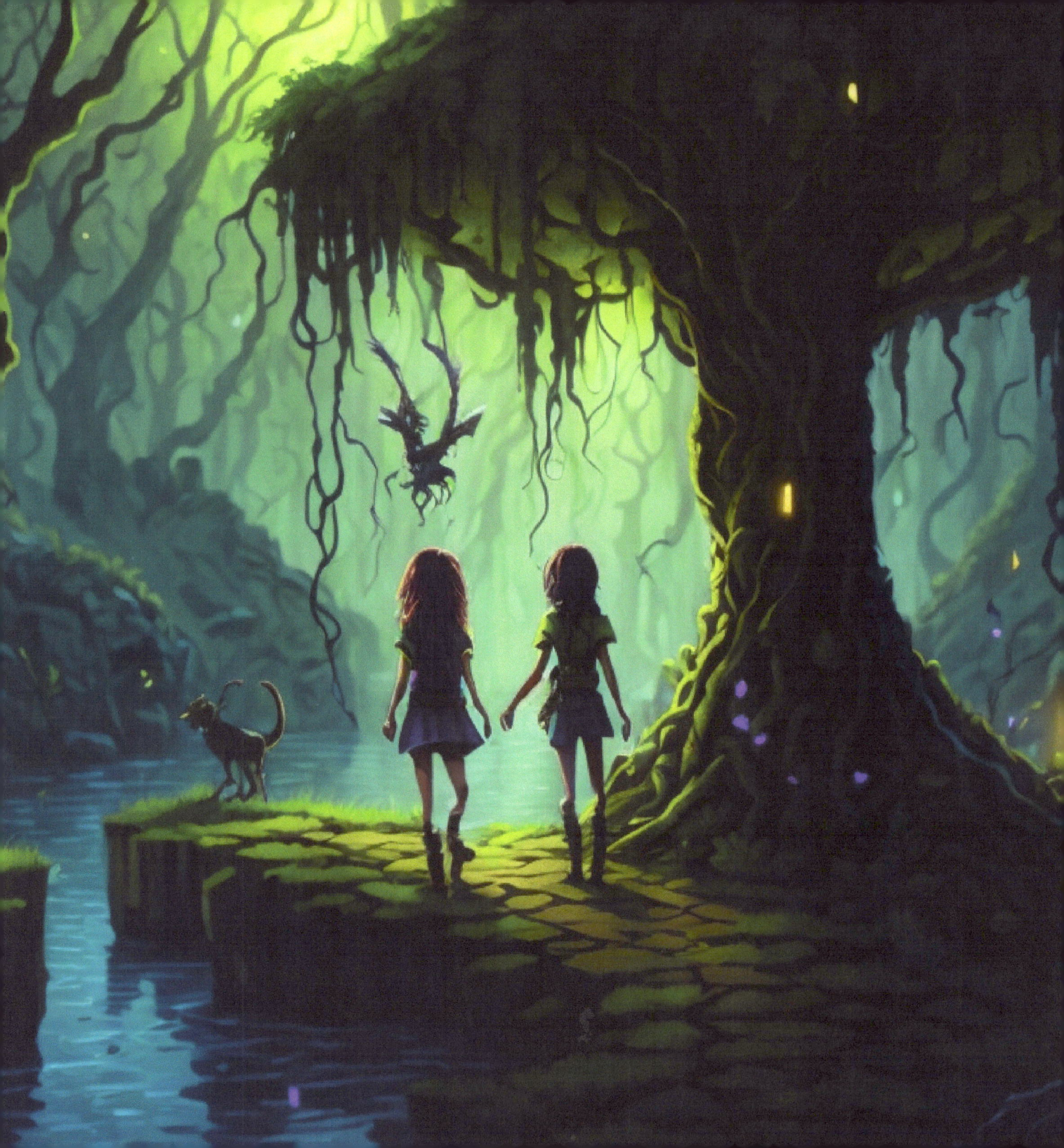

With the mischievous creature causing chaos in the enchanted forest, Willow and Wanda embark on a quest to find a solution. They encounter challenges and meet other magical beings who have been affected by the creature's antics. Along the way, the witches learn about responsibility and the importance of thinking before casting spells. The quest deepens their understanding of the magical world and the impact of their actions.

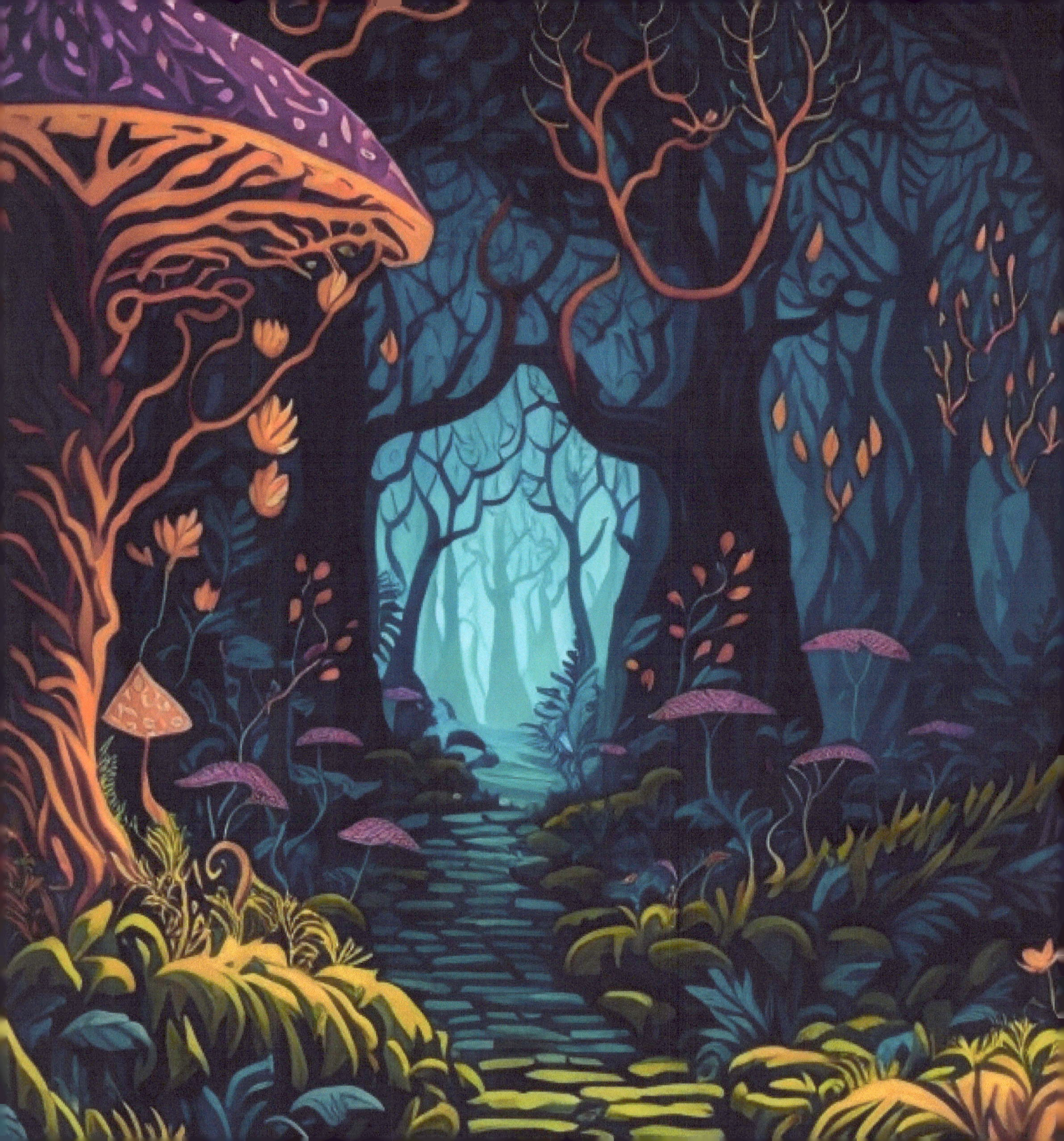

The Friendship Spell

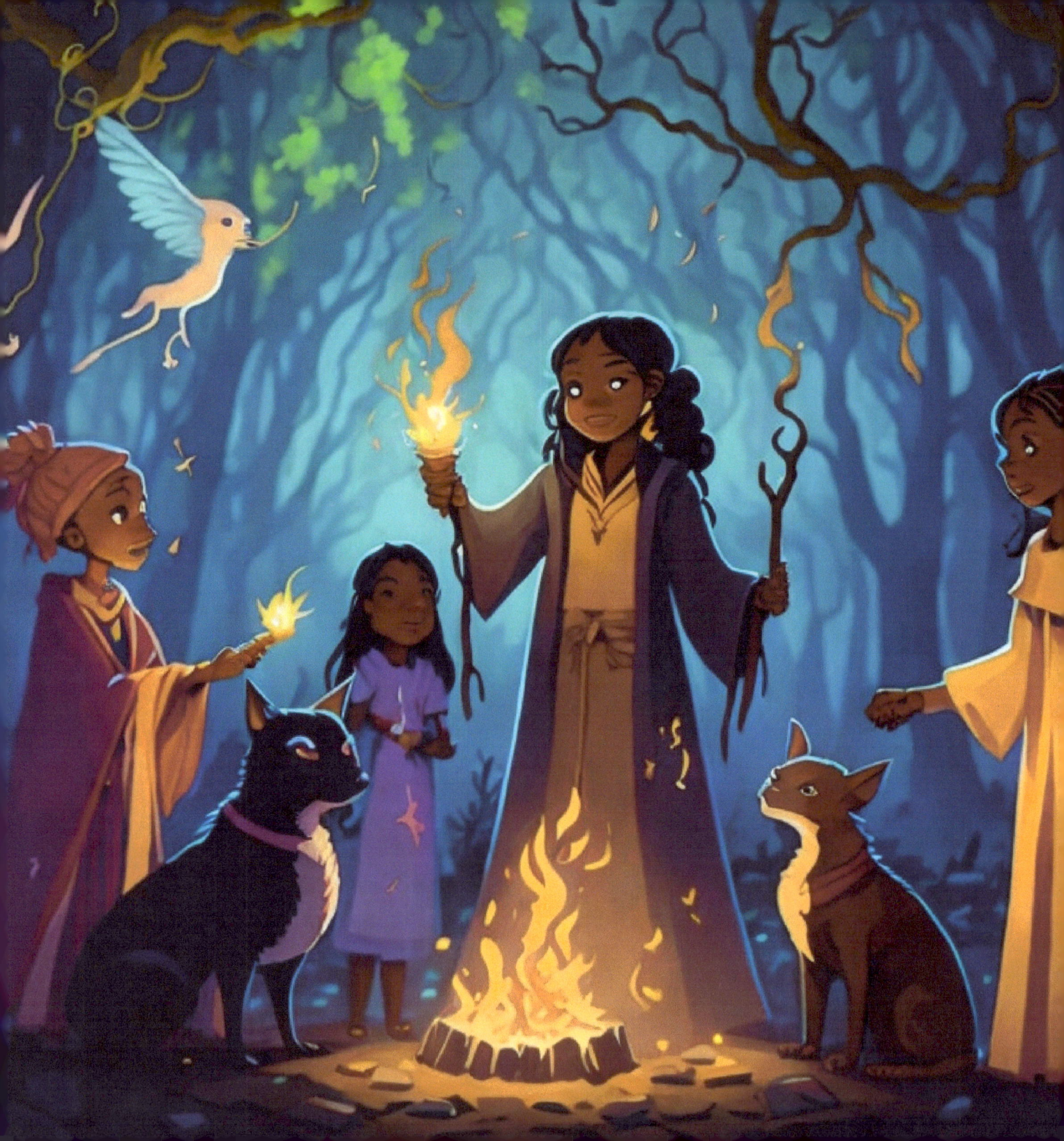

To capture the mischievous creature, Willow and Wanda need the help of other magical beings. They learn about a legendary Friendship Spell that can unite all magical creatures for a common cause. The witches, now wiser and more responsible, embark on a journey to cast the spell. This chapter emphasizes the themes of friendship and cooperation, showcasing the diversity of magical beings in the enchanted forest.

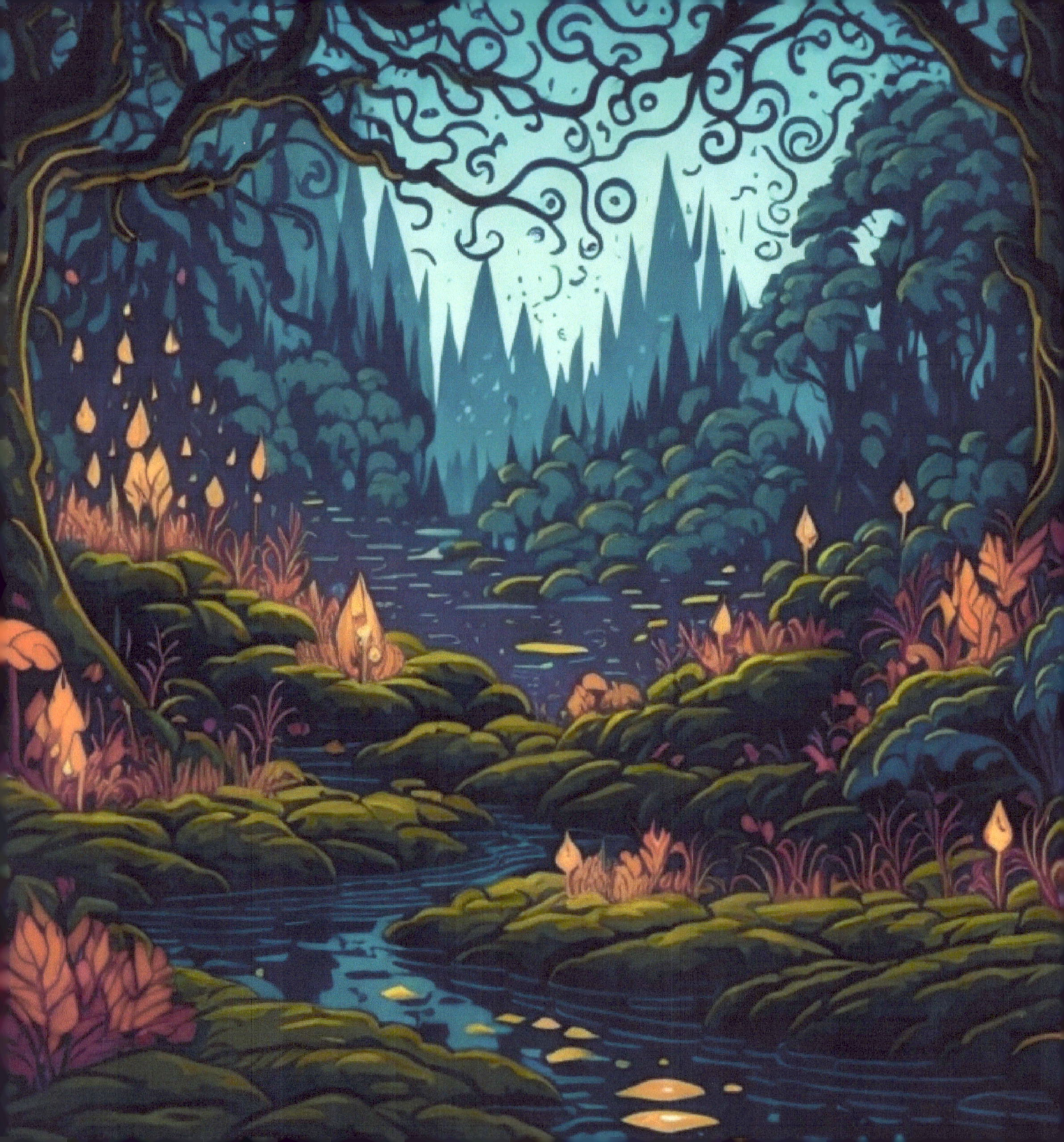

The Grand

Finale

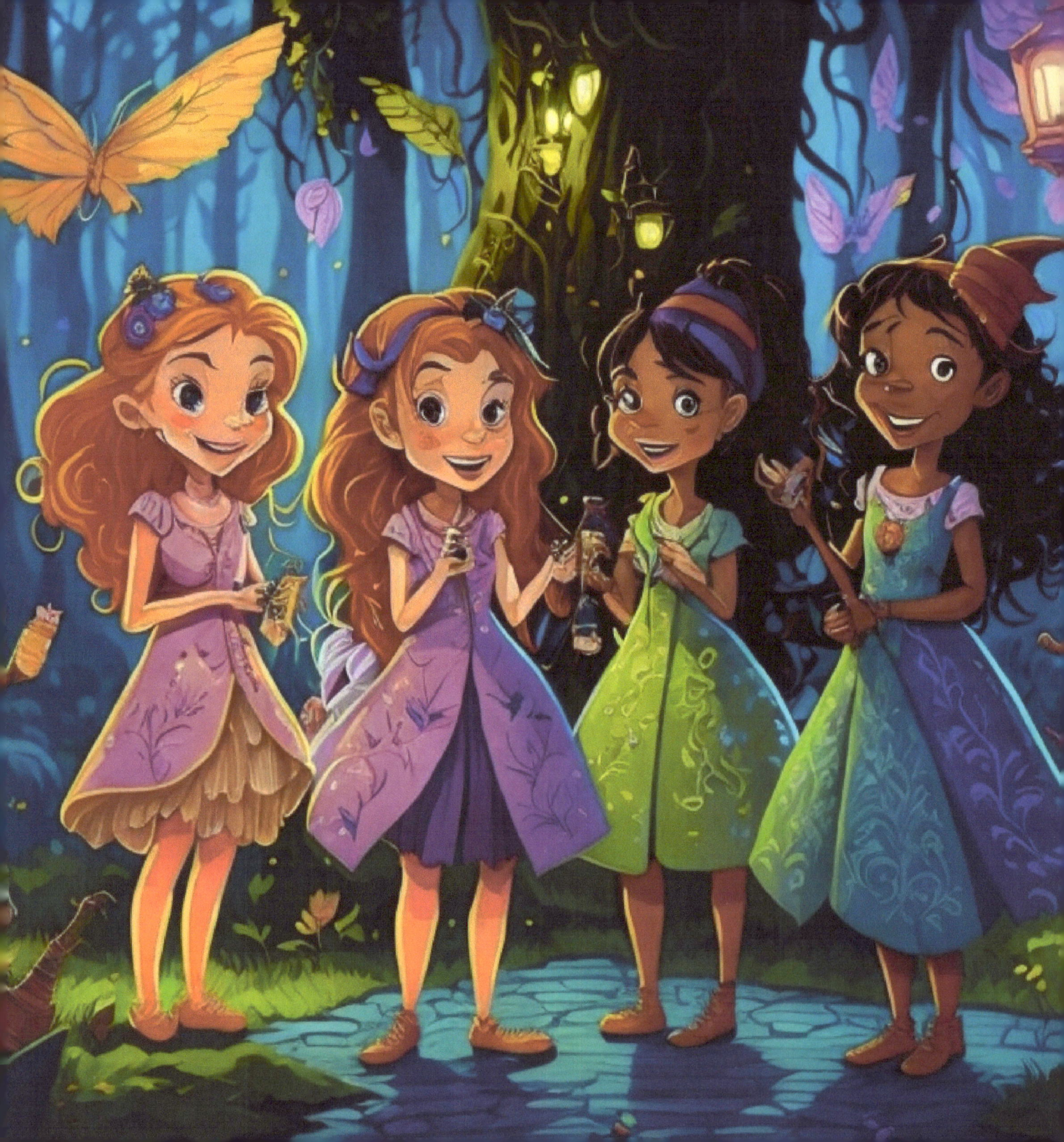

The witches, along with their newfound friends, devise a plan to capture the mischievous creature during a grand magical event in the forest. The plan unfolds in a series of comical events, showcasing the unique abilities of each magical being. The story concludes with a triumphant moment as the mischievous creature is captured, and Willow and Wanda earn the respect and admiration of their magical community. The chapter ends on a high note, celebrating the unity and teamwork of the magical beings.

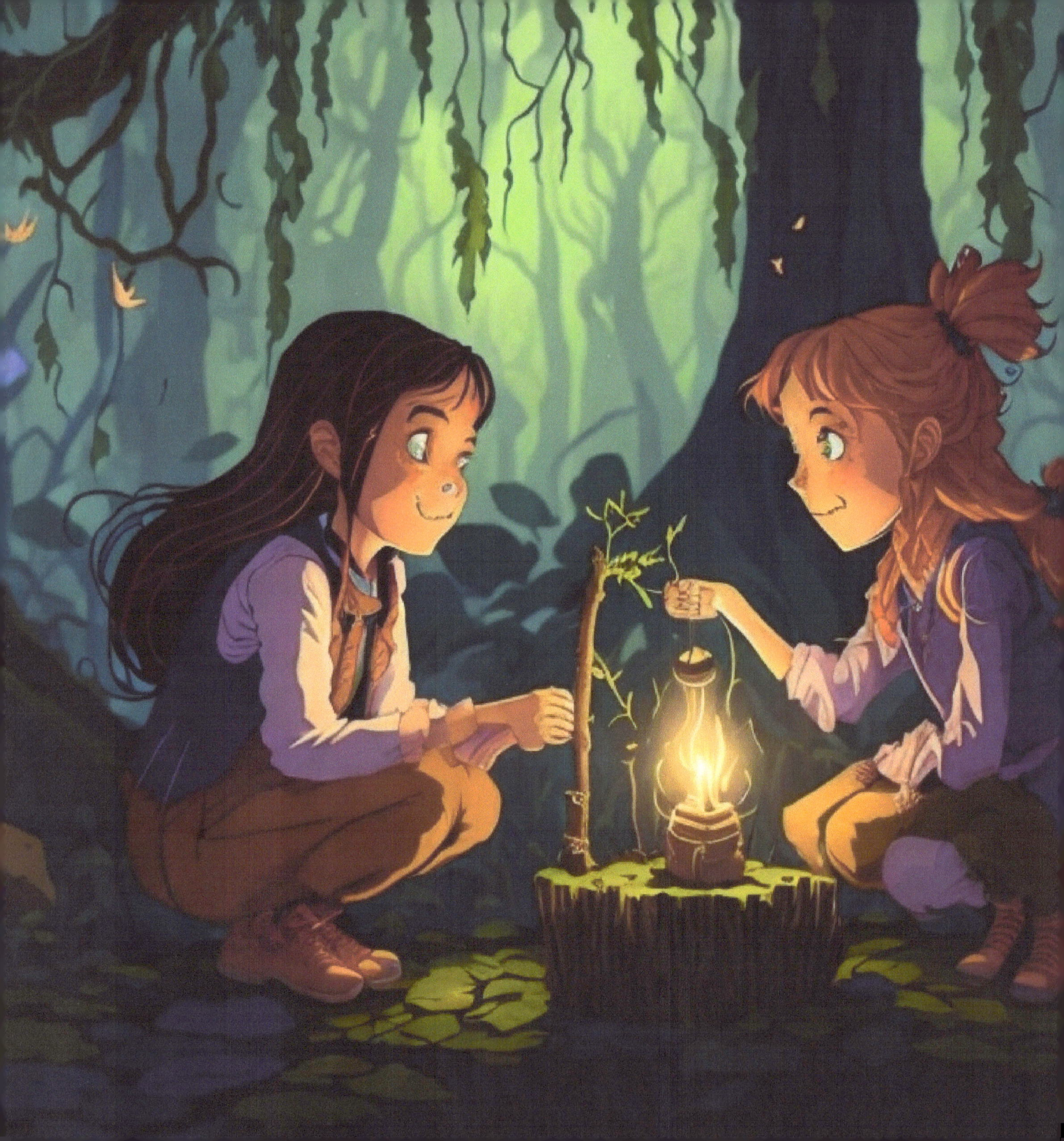